Table of Contents

*This book is dedicated to
Denise Comanne (1949–2010),
my partner in life and struggle*

Introduction

FROM THE 1970s to the world crisis of 2008–09,[1] neoliberal ideology conquered so many of our collective representations that it has largely dominated the political and economic thinking over the last three decades. Although it is currently being questioned, it is deeply embedded in the minds of opinion-makers and an overwhelming majority of decision-makers. Their reasoning has not fundamentally changed. But they also find it hard to assert that we must trust the self-regulating ability of corporation CEOs and financial markets.

The neoliberal ideology, which is simply the capitalist vision of the world doctored to the taste of the late twentieth and early twenty-first centuries, still prevails in universities, major economic journals, and the media. The new ideological kit for the next capitalist stage has not yet been produced on a mass scale. The approach developed before the crisis still holds good.

In 2009 and 2010, the public debt in the countries of the North literally exploded—the result was the financial rescue plans that incurred enormous costs for the treasuries of these countries. This steep rise in the public debt gave the neoliberal offensive a new impetus, favoring increased privatization to generate liquidities that would repay the debt, to the detriment of social spending and protection systems for people in countries where major mobilizations had formerly succeeded in protecting them to a significant extent. It is shocking to observe that in spite of the degeneration of neoliberal ideology and programs, the majority of governments in the North are currently reinforcing the neoliberal option.

At the start of the present crisis the deregulation policy fiasco was such that many commentators believed the governing classes would be obliged to put neo-Keynesian policies into practice. But what has happened up to now seems to contradict this prognosis. The fundamental reason for this is the weak state of the workers' fight for a new, more equitable distribution of income, together with the continued pursuit of a social-liberal approach on the part of the traditional left-wing parties, who either have gone along with the neoliberal offensive or failed to oppose it. At the end of 2009 and beginning of 2010, as the economic crisis affecting the industrialized world slackened its pace, the mainstream media and government spokesmen announced that the end of the tunnel was in view. But in reality the crisis is far from over. It will continue to produce its effects for several years to come.

In the countries of both the global North and the South, the jobs and incomes of the more modest categories of workers will come under major pressure in the name of repayment of the public debt. There is all the more reason for those who militate in the field to seek a common resistance uniting the oppressed of the North and the peoples of the South.

Right-wing governments as well as almost all social-liberal governments still apply the neoliberal ideology, or submit to it, with or without a sense of shame. Alan Greenspan, chairman of the US Federal Reserve from 1987 to 2006, explains in his autobiography how highly he thinks of Labor leaders such as Tony Blair and Gordon Brown for their adhesion to the neoliberal offensive:

In office from 1997 forward, Tony Blair and Gordon Brown, heads of a rejuvenated and far more centrist Labor Party, accepted Thatcher's profoundly important structural changes to British product and labor markets. In fact Brown, the chancellor of the exchequer for a record number of years, appeared to revel in Britain's remarkable surge of economic flexibility. (Brown encouraged my proselytizing to our G7 colleagues about the importance of flexibility to economic stability.) What socialism was left in twenty-first-century Britain was much reduced.... Britain's success with the free-market thrust of Thatcher and "New Labor" suggests that their GDP-enhancing reforms are likely to persevere through the next generation.

Britain's evolution from the ossified economy of the years immediately following the Second World War to one of the most open economies in the world is reflected in the intellectual journey of Gordon Brown, who described his education in an e-mail to me in 2007: "I came to economics principally through the concern about social justice my father taught me.... In the eighties, I saw that we needed a more flexible economy to create jobs. My understanding of an inclusive globalization is that we must combine stability, free trade, open markets, and flexibility with investment in equipping people for jobs of the future, principally through education. I hope in Britain we have prepared ourselves best for the global economic challenge, buttressing our policies for stability with a commitment to free trade, not protectionism."[2]

Although worn down to nothing, the neoliberal ideology still holds sway not only in the industrialized countries of the North, but also in Eastern Europe (Federation of Russia included) and in the Third World countries. Several governments in the South that formerly developed a socializing, or even a Moscow/Beijing inspired "Marxist-Leninist" kind of discourse in the 1960s and 70s have embraced it with the fervor of the newly converted.

But we should note that those who produce ideology and draft the speeches of the heads of state of the most industrialized countries have shifted their reasoning. The crisis that burst in the heart of the system bred a sort of chrysalis within some zealous servants of the system. The neoliberal larva wants to turn into a capitalist dragonfly. It wants to cast off its tattered grey suit and assume the motley appearance of a capitalist re-confection based on a subtle balance between freedom for capitalists and a sense of responsibility for the common good guaranteed by the state's wise regulation. Since the crisis is multidimensional with a strong environmental component in addition to its economic and financial aspects, one and all—from Barack Obama to Nicolas Sarkozy via Gordon Brown—harp upon a new "green capitalism."

Before analyzing the ideological foundations of the capitalist policies since the 1970s and 80s, it is useful to remember that other policies, distinctly removed from the "hands off" variety, were implemented in capitalist countries for decades during the twentieth century. The majority of them did indeed help maintain capitalism. But they contrasted with those that preceded the Wall Street crash in 1929 as well as with those that would be developed in Chile from 1973, in the UK from 1979, in the US from 1980, and that eventually prevailed almost everywhere.

A Glance in the Rearview Mirror

Liberalism Eclipsed: from the 1930s to the 1970s

ALTHOUGH A strong influence throughout the nineteenth century and the first third of the twentieth century, liberal thinking was eclipsed for a long period that lasted from the middle of the 1930s to the end of the 1970s.[1]

During the 1920s the financial markets had seemed irreversibly almighty. The crash in 1929 made it necessary for governments to strictly monitor financial and banking activities.

During this withdrawal of free trade prevalence (from the 1930s in North and South America and after the Second World War in Europe) various policies involving strong government intervention in the economy came to hold sway. This was true of the United States under Roosevelt's New Deal in the 1930s, and thirty years later under the J. F. Kennedy and L. B. Johnson administrations. It was true of France with the *Front populaire*, of Britain during the 1930s and just after the Second World War under Beveridge (advised by J. M. Keynes), and under subsequent Labor governments. After the Second World War, it was also true of France, Germany, the Netherlands, Belgium, and the Scandinavian countries. Keynesianism—whether of the Social Democratic, the "socialist," or the Social-Christian variety—dominated the economic thinking.

After the Second World War, private companies had been nationalized in Central and Eastern European countries, before they were labelled "popular democracies" and controlled by Moscow.

In a number of key Third World countries, developmentalist, nationalist, and even socialist policies came to the fore, as in China after the 1949 revolution. Anti-communist regimes in the Third World, such as the ones in South Korea and Taiwan, carried out radical agrarian reforms and built a strong government-controlled industrial sector. This is the central (and well-hidden) reason for the economic "miracle" that took place in those two "tiger" economies. The policies that created the past successes of South Korea and Taiwan stand in stark contrast to neoliberal prescriptions.[2] This point cannot be overemphasised.

The eclipse of liberalism came about as a result of the prolonged economic crisis that began with the Wall Street crash in 1929, and as a result of the victory of fascism and Nazism and their subsequent defeat at the hands of the masses (strikes and armed resistance) and of the Allied forces (United States, USSR, Britain, and France). The war and the defeat of fascism opened the way to significant political and social changes in the world. These began with concessions to the working class, the crisis of the colonial empires, and the liberation struggles of dominated Third World peoples. To this can be added the relative success of industrialization by import substitution in Latin America, the economic dynamism of India after it won independence from Britain in 1947, of Algeria after it won independence from France in 1962 to the 1970s, and of Egypt under Nasser in the 1950s and 1960s. There was also economic progress in the so-called socialist countries (in Eastern Europe after the war and in the USSR from the 1930s onwards).

This period shows a number of striking features. Firstly, a large number of private companies came under public control ("nationalization"), beginning in both Western and Eastern Europe in the wake of the victory over the Nazis and extending into the Third World until the mid-1970s. Secondly, social welfare systems were set up and expanded as part of what came to be known as the welfare state (from Roosevelt's New Deal to policies implemented in several Third World countries such as Mexico in the 1930s under Lazaro Cardenas). Thirdly, the economic model in place was "Fordist," in that it involved the development of mass consumption of durable goods in the industrialized countries. Fourthly, a social compromise was reached in these countries between the leadership of the labor movement (parties and trade unions) and "their" capitalist class. This compromise took the form of agreements contributing to social harmony. These features arose and prospered in a context of sustained growth—in the developed capitalist countries, the Third World, and the so-called socialist countries.

These wide-ranging political and economic developments also included a worldwide renewal of nondogmatic Marxism. In the developed capitalist countries we saw the publication of the works of Ernest Mandel, Paul Sweezy, Paul Baran, and André Gunder Frank, to name but a few.

In Cuba, after the revolutionary victory on January 1, 1959, came the works of Ernesto Che Guevara in the 1960s. In Eastern Europe, Kuron and Modzelewsky in the Poland of the 1960s, Karel Kosik, Rudolf Bahro, and others gave the foundation to a non-dogmatic Marxism that emerged in opposition to the fossilized Stalinist system.

It is also worth noting the emergence of the Marxist-influenced dependency school of thought in Latin America (Theotonio Dos Santos, Rui Mauro Marini, and Fernando Henrique Cardoso). Finally, there was the work of Samir Amin on de-linking.

Liberal Ideology[3] Returns with a Vengeance : The 1970s

LIBERAL IDEOLOGY returned with a vengeance in the 1970s, in response to the economic crisis in the main industrialized capitalist countries. The crisis marked the beginning of a long wave of slow growth, or rather a long downturn. The liberal counteroffensive picked up steam with the Third World debt crisis in the early 1980s and the implosion of the bureaucratic regimes of Eastern Europe at the end of the 1980s, followed by the restoration of capitalism in the former Soviet bloc and China.

This liberal (or neoliberal) resurgence has underlain and justified the massive worldwide offensive waged by capital against labor. This offensive began in the second half of the 1970s[4] in the industrialized capitalist countries. It continued with the progressive restoration of capitalism resulting from the collapse of the bureaucratic regimes of the East at the end of the 1980s. It included the crisis of the "developmentalist" models in the countries of the South, aggravated by the foreign debt crisis, leading to a new cycle of heightened dependence for countries that had experienced partially autonomous industrialization (such as Mexico, Argentina, Brazil, India, and Algeria). South Korea may soon join the ranks of these latter countries. As for the most dependent and least industrialized countries (in Central America; the Caribbean—except for Cuba; Sub-Saharan Africa; and South Asia—except for India), they never really escaped dependence on the North's capitalist powers. They are now fully under the thumb of the international financial institutions (including Nicaragua and Vietnam, which had indeed experienced authentic revolutions). Institutions such as the Economic Commission for Latin America (CEPAL) and the United Nations Conference on Trade and Development (UNCTAD) have slowly but surely joined the neoliberal chorus—though it is true that this process has not always been a smooth one. As for the Non-Aligned Movement (NAM), it has not survived the Yugoslav crisis, the Third World debt crisis, and the overall neoliberal offensive.

Neoliberal Ideology Is Not a Product of the Crisis

LIBERAL (or neoliberal) ideology is not a product of the crisis of the 1970s and early 1980s. It existed long before the crisis broke. A variety of economists and political leaders continued to identify with liberal ideas in spite of the preeminence of Keynesian and protosocialist policies. A number of them had long been sharpening their theoretical wits. They had been engaged in a wide-reaching ideological battle with the Keynesian ideas favored in the North, the "developmentalist" ideas in the South (personified by such people as CEPAL head Raul Prebisch for several decades), and with socialist and Marxist ideas in general in various parts of the world.

The Theoretical Foundation of the Various Neoliberal Currents

METHODOLOGICALLY SPEAKING, it is not easy to define the main tenets of neoliberal thought. The same goes for Keynesian and Marxist thought. Each one of these schools of thought has many different currents. There are profound differences between the different currents of liberalism, just as there are within Keynesianism and Marxism. There have also been attempts to synthesise liberal and post-Keynesian ideas, on the one hand, and liberal and post-Marxist ideas, on the other.

In general, the liberal (and neoliberal) school of thought is grounded in a vast and eclectic body of works—including neoclassical notions such as the quantitative theory of money, Say's law, the theory of prices based on the interaction of supply and demand, and the theory of comparative advantages....

The neoliberal ideology drew inspiration from economic, political, and philosophical theories which date back to David Hume (1711–76),

Adam Smith (1723–90), Jean-Baptiste Say (1767–1832), David Ricardo (1772–1823), even Emmanuel Kant (1724–1804).

Friedrich von Hayek (1899–1992) and Paul Samuelson are good examples of why it is so difficult to clearly define the parameters of neoliberalism. Hayek currently enjoys enormous popularity as an ultra-liberal, yet he rejects many key hypotheses of neoclassical thought. Samuelson does not belong to the liberal school, yet in the 1950s he pushed for a synthesis of neoclassical thought.

Forerunners of the Neoliberals

Adam Smith

Smith (*An Inquiry into the Nature and the Causes of the Wealth of Nations*, 1776) carried out a synthesis of the contributions of a number of schools of economic thought, including that of the French physiocrats. He opposed mercantilism, which had been responsible for two centuries of protectionism and state intervention. The main expressions of mercantilism were Colbertism in France, bullionism in Spain, and the policies of Cromwell and Petty in England. Adam Smith is best remembered for his allegory of the "invisible hand." According to Smith, every individual *"intends only his own gain, and he is in this, as in many other cases, led by an invisible hand to promote an end which was no part of his intention."*[5]

Here is the passage in which one can find Adam Smith's quote on the invisible hand:

> As every individual, therefore, endeavours as much as he can both to employ his capital in the support of domestic industry, and so to direct that industry that its produce may be of the greatest value; every individual necessarily labors to render the annual revenue of the society as great as he can. He generally, indeed, neither intends to promote the public interest, nor knows how much he is promoting it. By preferring the support of domestic to that of foreign industry, he intends only his own security; and by directing that industry in such a manner as its produce may be of the greatest value, he intends only his own gain, and he is in this, as in many other cases, led by an invisible hand to promote an end which was no part of his intention. Nor is it always the worse for the society that it was no part of it. By pursuing his own interest he frequently promotes that of the society more effectually than when he really intends to promote it. I have never known much good done by those who affected to trade for the public good. It is an affectation, indeed, not very common among merchants,

and very few words need be employed in dissuading them from it.[6]

In Smith's discourse, the invisible hand contrasts with the visible hand of the government which tries to regulate trade, industry, etc. Smith seeks to show how the intervention of the tangible hand of the state generally has negative results. For Smith, public spending should be limited to defense, justice, and public works when and where private entrepreneurs were not willing to take charge themselves, *"and which it therefore cannot be expected that any individual or small number of individuals should erect or maintain."*[7]

Adam Smith's ideas correspond to the development of strong English capitalism in the eighteenth century and laid part of the foundation for "economic liberalism."

We should recall that Smith has been a source of inspiration not only for liberals (and neoliberals). Some parts of his analysis (and that of the mercantilists he fought) were taken on by Karl Marx in his critique of political economy. Indeed, for Smith, *"Labor, therefore, is the real measure of the exchangeable value of all commodities."*[8] David Ricardo expanded on this notion, and Marx further developed it while acknowledging his debt to Smith and Ricardo. Unlike Smith, Marx also used a number of the mercantilists' contributions.[9]

On several essential points, Smith is closer to Karl Marx than those showering praise on Smith today. In the following citations, we discover that what Adam Smith wrote in the 1770s is not so distant from what Karl Marx and Friedrich Engels would write seventy years later in the famous *Communist Manifesto.* According to Adam Smith: "The labor of a manufacturer adds, generally, to the value of the materials which he works upon, that of his own maintenance, and of his master's profit."[10] In Marxist terms, this means that through their labor workers reproduce part of the constant capital[11] (the quantity of raw materials, energy, percentage of the value of the technical machinery, and so on, that are accounted for in the manufacturing of a given commodity) to which must be added the variable capital corresponding to their wages and the profit made by capitalists, which Karl Marx called surplus value.

Karl Marx and Adam Smith—each in his own time—both considered that it is the workers, not the bosses/capitalists, who produce value.

Workers create value, then, without in fact costing [their capitalist bosses] anything: "Though the manufacturer [i.e. the worker] has his wages advanced to him by his master, he, in reality, costs him [the capitalist] no expense, the value of those wages being generally restored, together with a profit, in the improved value of the subject upon which his labor is bestowed."[12]

In the following passage, Adam Smith analyzes the conflicts of interest and the class struggle opposing capitalists and workers:

What are the common wages of labor, depends everywhere upon the contract usually made between those two parties [workers and capitalists], whose interests are by no means the same. The workmen desire to get as much, the masters to give as little as possible. The former are disposed to combine in order to raise, the latter in order to lower the wages of labor.

It is not, however, difficult to foresee which of the two parties must, upon all ordinary occasions, have the advantage in the dispute, and force the other into a compliance with their terms. The masters, being fewer in number, can combine much more easily; and the law, besides, authorizes, or at least does not prohibit their combinations, while it prohibits those of the workmen. We have no acts of parliament against combining to lower the price of work; but many against combining to raise it. In all such disputes the masters can hold out much longer. A landlord, a farmer, a master manufacturer, a merchant, though they did not employ a single workman, could generally live a year or two upon the stocks which they have already acquired. Many workmen could not subsist a week, few could subsist a month, and scarce any a year without employment. In the long run the workman may be as necessary to his master as his master is to him; but the necessity is not so immediate.

We rarely hear, it has been said, of the combinations of masters, though frequently of those of workmen. But whoever imagines, upon this account, that masters rarely combine, is as ignorant of the world as of the subject. Masters are always and everywhere in a sort of tacit, but constant and uniform combination, not to raise the wages of labor above their actual rate. To violate this combination is everywhere a most unpopular action, and a sort of reproach to a master among his neighbours and equals. We seldom, indeed, hear of this combination, because it is the usual, and one may say, the natural state of things, which nobody ever hears of. Masters, too, sometimes enter into particular combinations to sink the wages of labor even below this rate. These are always conducted with the utmost silence and secrecy, till the moment of execution, and when the workmen yield, as they sometimes do, without resistance, though severely felt by them, they are never heard of by other people. Such combinations, however, are frequently resisted by a contrary defensive combination of the workmen; who sometimes too, without any provocation of this kind, combine of their own accord to raise the price of their labor. Their usual pretences are, sometimes the high price of provisions; sometimes the great profit which their masters make by their work. But whether their combinations be offensive or defensive, they are always abundantly heard of. In order to bring the point to a speedy decision, they have always recourse to the loudest clamour, and sometimes to the most shocking violence and outrage. They are desperate, and act with the folly and extravagance of desperate men, who must either starve, or frighten their masters into an immediate compliance with their demands. The masters upon these occasions are just as clamorous upon the other side, and never cease to call aloud for the assistance of the civil magistrate, and the rigorous execution of those laws which have been enacted with so much severity against the combinations of servants, laborers, and journeymen.[13]

According to Adam Smith, this state of things motivates the capitalist as follows:

The consideration of his own private profit is the sole motive which determines the owner of any capital to employ it either in agriculture, in manufactures, or in some particular branch of the wholesale or retail trade. The different quantities of productive labor which it may put into motion, and the different values which it may add to the annual produce of the land and labor of the society, according as it is employed in one or other of those different ways, never enter into his thoughts.[14]

Adam Smith argues that there are three basic social classes: 1) landowners, who live by renting their land; 2) wage earners; and 3) capitalists, who live off the profits they make. Smith describes the class consciousness and class interests of these three social groups in his own terms:

The whole annual produce of the land and labor of every country, or what comes to the same thing, the whole price of that annual produce, naturally divides itself, it has already been observed, into three parts; the rent of land, the wages of labor, and the profits of stock; and constitutes a revenue to three different orders of people; to those who live by rent, to those who live by wages, and to those who live by profit. These are the three great, original, and constituent orders of every civilised society, from whose revenue that of every other order is ultimately derive. . . .

Speaking of the class that has its own private means, that is, the landowners, Adam Smith asserts that:

They are the only one of the three orders whose revenue costs them neither labor nor care, but comes to them, as it were, of its own accord, and independent of any plan or project of their own. That indolence, which is the natural effect of the ease and security of their situation, renders them too often, not only ignorant, but incapable of that application of mind which is necessary in order to foresee and understand the consequences of any public regulation.

The interest of the second order, that of those who live by wages, is as strictly connected with the interest of the society as that of the first. . . .

But though the interest of the laborer is strictly connected with that of the society, he is incapable either of comprehending that interest or of understanding its connection with his own. His condition leaves him no time to receive the necessary information, and his education and habits are commonly such as to render him unfit to judge even though he was fully informed. In the public deliberations, therefore, his voice is little heard and less regarded, except upon some particular occasions, when his clamour is animated, set on and supported by his employers, not for his, but their own particular purposes.

His employers constitute the third order, that of those who live by profit. It is the stock that is employed for the sake of profit which puts into motion the greater part of the useful labor of every society. The plans and projects of the employers of stock regulate and direct all the most important operations of labor, and profit is the end proposed by all those plans and projects. . . . Merchants and master manufacturers are, in this order, the two classes of people who commonly employ the largest capitals, and who by their wealth draw to themselves the greatest share of the public consideration. As during their whole lives they are engaged in plans and projects, they have frequently more acuteness of understanding than the greater part of country gentlemen. . . .

The interest of the dealers, however, in any particular branch of trade or manufactures, is always in some respects different from, and even opposite to, that of the public. To widen the market and to narrow the competition, is always the interest of the dealers. To widen the market may frequently be agreeable enough to the interest of the public; but to narrow the competition must always be against it, and can serve only to enable the dealers, by raising their profits above what they naturally would be, to levy, for their own benefit, an absurd tax upon the rest of their fellow-citizens. The proposal of any new law or regulation of commerce which comes from this order ought always to be listened to with great precaution, and ought never to be adopted till after having been long and carefully examined, not only with the most scrupulous, but with the most suspicious attention. It comes from an order of men whose interest is never exactly the same with that of the public, who have generally an interest to deceive and even to oppress the public, and who accordingly have, upon many occasions, both deceived and oppressed it.[15]

Smith's works contain other similar judgments, which would give rashes to those politicians and ideologists who claim to be his disciples: "Our merchants frequently complain of the high wages of British labor as the cause of their manufactures being undersold in foreign markets, but they are silent about the high profits of stock. They complain of the extravagant gain of other people, but they say nothing of their own. The high profits of British stock, however, may contribute towards raising the price of British manufactures in many cases as much, and in some perhaps more, than the high wages of British labor."[16] This statement would be a heresy for the capitalists, who hold wage costs—always too high in their opinion—responsible for inflation and the lack of competitiveness.

These concepts, which are as essential (if not more) in the thought of Adam Smith as the famous invisible hand (only mentioned three times in his work), are systematically forgotten by today's dominant economic thinkers.[17]

One of the fundamental differences between Adam Smith and Karl Marx, is that the former, although he was conscious of how workers are exploited by capitalists, supported the capitalists whereas the latter argued for the emancipation of workers.

The General Rules of the International Workingmen's Association 1864 (IWA[18]) written by Karl Marx express the basic substance of his position:

Considering,

That the emancipation of the working classes must be conquered by the working classes themselves, that the struggle for the emancipation of the working classes means not a struggle for class privileges and monopolies, but for equal rights and duties, and the abolition of all class rule;

That the economical subjection of the man of labor to the monopolizer of the means of labor — that is, the source of life — lies at the bottom of servitude in all its forms, of all social misery, mental degradation, and political dependence;

That the economical emancipation of the working classes is therefore the great end to which every political movement ought to be subordinate as a means;

That all efforts aiming at the great end hitherto failed from the want of solidarity between the manifold divisions of labor in each country, and from the absence of a fraternal bond of union between the working classes of different countries;

That the emancipation of labor is neither a local nor a national, but a social problem, embracing all countries in which modern society exists, and depending for its solution on the concurrence, practical and theoretical, of the most advanced countries;

That the present revival of the working classes in the most industrious countries of Europe, while it raises a new hope, gives solemn warning against a relapse into the old errors, and calls for the immediate combination of the still disconnected movements;

For these reasons —

The International Working Men's Association has been founded.

It declares:

That all societies and individuals adhering to it will acknowledge truth, justice, and morality as the basis of their conduct toward each other and toward all men, without regard to color, creed, or nationality;

That it acknowledges no rights without duties, no duties without rights.[19]

Jean-Baptiste Say

In 1803, Say described a law whereby the role of money is neutral in the economy and "supply creates its own demand." Therefore, no crisis of overproduction is possible in a free market economy.

Say's law is a key reference for liberal (and neoliberal) economists. Yet it was proved wrong by events in Say's time, a point that has been raised by a wide range of economists from Malthus (1820, *Principles of Political Economy: Considered with a View to Their Practical Application*) to Sismondi (1819, *Nouveaux principes d'économie politique ou de la richesse dans ses rapports avec la population*, Calman-Lévy,1971) and Marx.

David Ricardo

In his theory of competitive advantages (Ricardo, 1817, chapter VII "On Foreign Trade"), Ricardo critically takes and enhances Smith's stance in favor of free trade and an international division of labor. For Ricardo, a country does well to specialize in those areas of production whose relative costs are the lowest—in other words, those areas where it has the greatest comparative advantage. Unlike Smith, he goes on to say that countries that have competitive advantages in all areas of production should nonetheless specialize.

"In a well-known example, Ricardo shows that if Portugal is more efficient than England in the production of both wine and fabric, it should still abandon the latter if its price advantage in wine production is greater. Inversely, England should specialize in the production of fabric, where its handicap is the least great."[20] The example referred to is to be found in chapter VII cited above.

Other economists

Today's neoliberals draw inspiration not only from Smith, Say, and Ricardo, but also from other economists such as Jevons (*The Theory of Political Economy*, 1871), Menger (*Grundsätze des Volkwirtschaftlehre*, 1871), and Walras (*Eléments d'économie politique pure ou théorie de la richesse sociale*, 1874–77.

These economists criticise both Ricardo's (and Marx's) analysis of value and his analysis of distribution. They developed a theory of prices based on the principle of decreasing marginal utility. Dominant economic thought refers to this theory as signalling the "marginalist revolution."

Within this framework, Walras also developed a theory postulating a system of general equilibrium. This theory is very much in vogue among today's neoliberals. In such a system, society is defined as a natural mechanism (akin to a biological organism and the solar system) within which individuals freely ensure the most effective allocation of resources, thereby guaranteeing optimum economic performance.

To complete the list of references for today's neoliberals, we must add the quantitative theory of money. This theory can be found in Smith's and Ricardo's works and has been around since at least the sixteenth century. It explains price movements as being a result of the quantity of money in circulation.

Taken together, all these references are described by some economists as forming a "neoclassical" synthesis. As Michel Beaud and Gilles Dostaler have pointed out, "Through it all, real life has persistently contradicted the analysis of many classical and neoclassical economists whereby the free functioning of the markets is enough to guarantee the full use of resources and their optimum allocation."[21]

Marxist scholars, beginning with Marx and Engels themselves, refuted the different component parts of this rather eclectic body of theoretical work at a time when Marxism influenced a large part of the international working-class movement.

By his own admission Keynes himself had originally championed the liberal cause. Yet seventy-five years after Marx and Engels, he developed a radical critique of a number of the central tenets in the classical (liberal) economic creed. In response to Smith and Say,[22] for example (and like Marx), he highlights the important contributions of the mercantilists. However, he stood by the liberal creed on a number of other matters—on such key questions, for example, as the definition of real salaries as being equal to the marginal productivity of labor.[23]

The Keynesian Revolution

A S A RESULT of the Depression of the 1920s and 1930s, a new wave of critics tackled the neoclassical creed on a largely pragmatic basis. This new wave was international and involved political leaders and economists from differing backgrounds belonging to various currents: enlightened bourgeois thinkers, socialists, and Marxists. In a context of mass unemployment and depression, proposals came forward for major public works, for anticyclical injections of public money, and even for bank expropriations. Such proposals came from a wide variety of sources: Germany's Doctor Schacht; the Belgian socialist Deman; the founders of the Stockholm School, backed by the Swedish social democrats; Fabian socialists and J. M. Keynes in Britain; J. Tinbergen in the Netherlands; Frisch in Norway; the Groupe X-Crise in France; Mexican president Lazaro Cardenas (1935–40); adepts of Peronism in the Argentina of the 1930s; and US president Roosevelt (elected in November 1932) and his New Deal.

The entire range of proposals and pragmatic policies was partially summed up in Keynes's 1936 work *General Theory of Employment, Interest and Money.*

The preparatory work carried out by Keynes (1883–1946), laying the groundwork for the *General Theory,* was fuelled by the need to find a solution to the spreading crisis of the capitalist system. Moreover, this solution had to be compatible with the continued survival of the system. The work was partially the result of a wide-ranging collective process wherein groups and individuals ended up in different Keynesian camps, often very much at odds with one another. Some leaned more towards Marxist positions, such as the Briton Joan Robinson and the Pole Michal Kalecki, who had actually formulated the key components of the *General Theory* before Keynes. Others grew progressively closer to the very tenets of liberalism and neoclassical economics that Keynes decried.

In one of his works, Keynes pays homage to the English philosopher George Edward Moore, whom he credits with having freed him from the prevailing morality of the day and having "protected us all from that *final reductio ad absurdum* of Benthamism known as Marxism."[24]

Keynes had been politically active since the First World War. As an employee of the British Exchequer, he actively participated in negotiations on the Treaty of Versailles, which marked the end of the war in 1918. He resigned from the British delegation in protest against the scale of reparations imposed on Germany. Soon after, he wrote *The Eco-*

nomic Consequences of the Peace (Keynes, 1919).

In the 1926 pamphlet *The End of Laissez-Faire*, he writes: "It is in no way accurate to deduce from the principles of political economy that enlightened personal interest always works in favour of the general interest."[25]

In the 1920s, Keynes condemned the policies of Winston Churchill's Tory government. He opposed the liberal (neoclassical) policies that provoked the miners' strike, followed by the 1926 General Strike.

Thereafter, he called for a policy of major public investment. He supported the Liberal Party while maintaining friendly ties with the Labor Party. In 1929, in the wake of the Tories' and Liberals' defeat, the new Labor government appointed him to the McMillan Commission on the economic situation. In 1930, he became an advisor to the same government.

The economic crisis deepened following the 1929 Wall Street crash, leading Keynes to produce an analysis of employment, interest, and money which strengthened his conviction that there should be increased state intervention. To compensate for the shortfall in demand, the state should increase spending in order to give a boost to the economy and employment.

Thereafter he became involved in a major debate with Hayek. Although, like Keynes, Hayek had come to reject a number of the ideas of Smith, Ricardo, Walras, and Jevons, with Ludwig von Mises (1881–1973) he fashioned a set of ultraliberal ideas which fiercely opposed the main tenets of the Keynesian revolution.

Whereas Keynes and his fellow economists were convinced that the Great Depression had been caused by the collapse in investment, Hayek and his supporters saw overinvestment rooted in slack monetary policies as the cause. For Keynes, consumption and investment had to be sparked by strong state intervention. For Hayek, state intervention reduced the funds available for private investment. For Keynes, wages had to be increased to stimulate consumption. For Hayek, they had to be lowered to ensure renewed full employment. The debate hit the pages of the British press in 1932 (*Times*, October 17 and 19, 1932).

Keynes believed that economic policy should be geared towards reducing the high unemployment rate and distributing revenues in a more egalitarian manner. If the government did not pursue the objectives of full employment and greater equality, he argued, there was a serious danger that either fascism or Bolshevik communism would win the day. Government policy had to be aimed at reducing high interest rates, which channelled vital resources into the financial sector.

By lowering interest rates, the aim was to favour the "euthanasia of the rentiers," the scourge of the capitalist system. At the same time, however, Keynes states quite clearly that the consequences of his theory are "moderately liberal": ". . . while it highlights the vital importance of establishing certain central controls in fields that today remain completely in the hands of private initiative, it also leaves a great many fields of activity in private hands [. . .] It does not actually call for a system of state socialism that would subject most of the community's economic life to its control."[26]

Keynes's prescriptions were put into practice in many regions of the world right up until the 1970s. They also strongly influenced a number of economists, such as Samuelson, Galbraith, Tobin, and Prebisch.

Preparing the Neoliberal Counterrevolution

THERE WAS a swift reaction to the policies of state intervention aimed at boosting demand and moving towards full employment. From the beginning of the 1930s, Hayek and von Mises set out to demolish Keynes's proposals. "Since 1945, in various academic and business circles, different projects have emerged simultaneously to bring together the qualified defenders of liberalism (neo-classical economics) with the aim of organizing a joint response to the advocates of state intervention and socialism. Three centres where this post-War resistance was organized were: the Institut universitaire de hautes études internationales (IUHEI) in Geneva, the London School of Economics (LSE) and the University of Chicago."[27]

At the end of the Second World War, Hayek was teaching at the LSE. In 1947, he and von Mises founded the Société du Mont-Pèlerin. The first meeting was held in April 1947 and brought together thirty-six liberal luminaries at the Hôtel du Parc at Mont-Pèlerin near Vevey in Switzerland. The gathering was financed by Swiss bankers and industrialists. Three major US publications (*Fortune, Newsweek,* and *Reader's Digest*) sent delegates. In fact, *Reader's Digest* had just run an abridged version of one of Hayek's main works, *The Road to Serfdom*. Among other things, that book said: "In the past, man's submission to the impersonal forces of the market made possible the development of a civilisation which otherwise would not have emerged. It is through submission that we participate every day in the building of something much bigger than what we can all fully understand."[28]

Right-wing economists and philosophers from different "schools of thought" participated in the gathering. "At the end of the meeting, the Société du Mont-Pèlerin was founded—a kind of neoliberal Freemasonry, very well organized and devoted to the dissemination of the neoliberal creed, with regular international gatherings."[29]

Among the organization's most active members were Hayek, von Mises, Maurice Allais, Karl Popper, and Milton Friedman. It became a think tank for the neoliberal counteroffensive. Many of its members went on to win the Nobel Prize in economics (Hayek in 1974, Friedman in 1976, and Allais in 1988).

The Neoliberal Wave

THE neoliberal current made the University of Chicago one of its bastions. Friedman spent his entire academic career there, while Hayek taught there between 1950 and 1961. Later on, people began to refer to the neoliberals as the Chicago School, and spoke of Friedman's "Chicago Boys." From 1970, Friedman declared that he had seen through the victory of the "counter-revolution in monetary theory," defined by him as the "renewed accent placed on the role of the quantity of money."[30] In his book *The Counter-revolution in Monetary Theory*, Friedman argues that all variations in the money supply are followed by corresponding changes in prices, production, and revenues. He says this law has been observed for centuries and can be compared to the laws of natural science. He concludes that the state cannot boost demand through the creation of money, lest unemployment rise in the same proportions. He proposes a constitutional amendment whereby the money supply should change at a constant rate, equal to the long-term rate of growth of national production.[31]

Following in the footsteps of Say, Friedman argues that the free functioning of the market is enough to ensure the optimum allocation of resources and the full use of production capacity. This view has been refuted by real life, but this has not stopped it from gaining wide recognition as a matter of "common sense."

Friedman did not remain aloof from politics; he put himself squarely in the reactionary camp. In 1964, he was economic advisor to Republican presidential candidate Barry Goldwater. He held the same post alongside Richard Nixon in 1968 and Ronald Reagan in 1980.

After the government of Salvador Allende was overthrown by a mil-

itary coup in Chile in 1973, he was advisor to general Pinochet. He supported the repression that was carried out and called for measures of
extreme austerity. Michel Beaud and Gilles Dostaler add, "In 1977, Milton Friedman produced a publication called *Against Galbraith*, based
on conferences given in Great Britain. In one such conference, he proposed that Great Britain, in order to solve its problems, should use a
form of shock therapy, such as the method used in Chile, which was
an example to aspire to."[32] Hayek also expressed support for the general's dictatorial and bloodthirsty methods. In response to a Chilean
journalist's questions in 1981, he said: "A dictator may rule in a liberal
way, just as it is possible for a democracy to rule without the slightest
liberalism. My personal preference is for a liberal dictatorship rather
than a democratic government thoroughly lacking in liberalism."[33]
After ten years of application of his economic policies, Chile entered a
recession that saw its GDP plummet by 15 percent in 1982–83, and unemployment of 30 percent.[34] Indeed, Chile was only able to become
something of an economic success story in the 1990s by breaking
cleanly with the approach of the "Chicago Boys."

While Ronald Reagan was inspired by Friedman, Margaret Thatcher
was a disciple of Hayek. "It was only in the middle of the 1970s, when
Hayek's works figured prominently in the readings that Keith Joseph
[Thatcher's economic advisor and participant at Mont-Pèlerin meet-
ings] gave me that I really grasped his ideas. It was only at that point
that I considered his arguments from the point of view of the type of
state dear to Conservatives (a limited government based on the rule of
law), as opposed to the point of view of the type of state to be avoided
(a socialist state where bureaucrats ruled unchecked)."[35]

If one looks carefully, from September 11, 1973, Chile became the
testing ground in the southern hemisphere where the neoliberal project was implemented in a particularly violent and brutal manner. After
the Chilean experiment of Augusto Pinochet's dictatorship, the neoliberal project was implemented in the northern hemisphere, starting
with Great Britain and the United States. Of course, the methods of im-
plementation differed but the social and economic orientation remained identical. The ideological reference points were the same.

Robert Lucas and the Denial of Involuntary Unemployment

The neoliberal counterrevolution has added a whole new dimension to reactionary ideas.

According to Robert Lucas, who describes himself as a partisan of "new classical macroeconomics," involuntary unemployment does not exist. For Keynes, the existence of involuntary unemployment was a given. However, according to Lucas, unemployment is caused by the choices a worker makes between work and leisure. Lucas argues that any economist seeking to understand changes in the labor market, must postulate that workers make rational choices between the amount of work time and leisure time. In other words, an unemployed worker is a person who has chosen to increase leisure time, even if this means their revenues fall or disappear.

The IMF and the Nonexistence of Involuntary Unemployment

ACCORDING TO Joseph Stiglitz, winner of the 2001 Nobel Prize for economics, the doctrine of the nonexistence of involuntary unemployment is still deeply ingrained within the International Monetary Fund (IMF).

In some of the universities from which the IMF hires regularly, the core curricula involve models in which there is never any unemployment. After all, in the standard competitive model—the model that underlies the IMF's market fundamentalism—demand always equals supply. If the demand for labor equals supply, there is never any involuntary unemployment. Someone who is not working has evidently chosen not to work. . . . While these models might provide some amusement within academia, they seem particularly ill-suited to understanding the problems of a country like South Africa, which has been plagued with unemployment rates in excess of 25 percent since apartheid was dismantled.

The IMF economists could not, of course, ignore the existence of unemployment. Because under market fundamentalism . . . there cannot be unemployment, the problem cannot lie with markets. It must lie elsewhere—with greedy unions and politicians interfering with the workings of free markets, by demanding—and getting—excessively high wages. There is an obvious policy implication—if there is unemployment, wages should be reduced.[36]

In line with the classical orthodoxy targeted by both Marx and Keynes, Lucas argues that there is a natural rate of unemployment, and that it is counterproductive for governments to seek to influence this rate with pump-priming job creation measures.

Lucas is a professor at the University of Chicago; in 1995, his contribution to the neoliberal offensive was rewarded with the Nobel Prize for economics.

He and his colleagues made a radical critique of Reagan's policies, rightly arguing that they had strayed from monetarist orthodoxy. They approved Reagan's monetarist plans to reduce the money supply; but said that tax cuts and high military spending—which could only widen the public deficit—were incompatible with this objective. They backed cuts in social spending and opposed the increase in military spending.

There was nothing ethical about their opposition to military spending, yet it revealed the striking incoherence between Reagan's monetarist convictions and his actual policies involving an increase in the public deficit. He partially applied Keynesian methods to get the United States out of recession with an increase in public spending. He did so in a reactionary manner, channelling the increased public funds into arms spending (and space research for the Strategic Defense Initiative—or Star Wars—project). As far as the interests of US imperialism were concerned, Reagan's approach—much criticised by the neoliberal keepers of the faith—ended up serving them quite well. The social costs, however, have been enormous.

The Absurdities of Neoliberal and Neoclassical Thought

THE IMPERIALISM of neoclassical economics (excerpts from Beaud and Dostaler, La pensée économique depuis Keynes, 183–85)

Neo-classical theory has long been criticised for its reductionism, which makes it unable to take into account the complexities of the world in which we live. Paradoxically, some neoclassical theorists linked to the Chicago School have reacted to this critique by pushing their reductionism to the extreme—making their theory the key to all knowledge of all social phenomena. The other social sciences—such as sociology, political science, history, and psychology—are seen as superfluous.

According to this view of things, society is a collection of independent agents (individuals, households, and companies). Each agent has free will; it is the interaction of the different individual decisions that determines the course of economic, social, and political life. Each agent is subjected to a series of constraints, both cognitive and material in nature. The resources available to each agent (goods and services, productive resources, information) are limited. Behavior can be foreseen based on the hypothesis that each agent will act rationally. This hypothesis, in fact, is the core of neoclassical analysis.

The big step was taken by Becker (who won the Nobel Prize for economics in 1992) and Mincer, both from the Chicago School. They have applied this approach, based on the rational behavior of each independent agent, to all human activities. This enables them to explain all human behavior, including criminal activities. Such activities, like all others, are seen to be the result of a rational calculation, wherein profits (high and short-term) are compared to costs (the danger of being apprehended and punished). Becker and his colleagues have generalized this analysis to include marriage, childbearing and rearing, divorce, and the division of household chores. In each case, it is a matter of making a rational cost-benefit analysis. The emergence of such specialities as the "new economy of the family" (Becker, 1968; Becker and Landes, 1974) shows how wide the net of *homo economicus* and rational choices has been cast.

In addition to being called "revolutionary," these changes have also been labelled "imperialist" (Stigler, 1984). The further afield Becker and his colleagues travel, the less room there is for genuine research in anthropology, psychology, political science, sociology, and all the social sciences and humanities—for this approach to economics sees itself as a general theory for all human behavior: "There is only one social science. What gives the economic sciences their capacity for imperialist expansion is the fact that our analytical categories—scarcity, cost, preference, opportunity—are truly universally applicable. . . . In this way, the economic sciences are the universal grammar of social science."[37]

Free Markets Ensure the Optimum Allocation of Resources—
A Key Postulate of Neoconservatism

"For the hand to remain invisible, the eye must be blind."[38]

OF COURSE, it is easy to argue that there is no example of a fully free-functioning market. This is obviously true in those countries where the authorities and organized workers refuse neoliberal dogmas and have managed to defend their social welfare system and retain reasonably stable employment and intact public services. Yet it is also true in all those countries where neoliberal policies have been implemented most aggressively. The neoliberals in power in the United States since 1980 have indeed cut back on what they see as obstacles to the free functioning of the market—for example, by diminishing the strength of the trade union movement and rolling back social welfare. But they have also strengthened other such "obstacles": through the greater concentration of companies, creating oligopolies in certain sectors; through the privatization of state-owned companies, eliminating any form of democratic control; through maintaining protectionism against foreign competitors (tariff barriers and other constraints on the free market); through strengthening the power of financial players, leading towards a "tyranny of the markets"; through restricting the free circulation of labor; and through a multiplicity of acts of financial delinquency that obstruct the working of the free market (one need merely look at the several scandals since the Enron debacle right up to Bernard Madoff's Ponzi pyramid scheme).

Meanwhile, in the case of the United States, inequalities have increased and poverty affects a larger portion of the population. A significant share of new jobs are poorly paid and short term. The prison population rose from 250,000 in 1975 to 744,000 in 1985, reaching 2.3 million in June 2008 (half of whom are African American or Latin American). Never before have there been so many economic activities of a criminal character by company heads and public officials—encouraged by the deregulation of capital flows.

In defense of their record, neoliberals always retort that resources are not optimally allocated since there is nowhere that the market functions unfettered. The task, therefore, is to struggle against obstacles to the market in view of achieving universal prosperity at some point in the distant future.

In fact, in the name of the quest for a free market (the neoliberal Promised Land), the objective is to destroy the gains of workers and the oppressed generally—gains which are described as so many reactionary "rigidities."

Portraying the Oppressed as Oppressors: The Neoliberal Sleight of Hand

IN FACT, there is nothing new about this line of argument. The idea is to single out the trade union movement and legislation defending workers as oppressive mechanisms. These mechanisms, the argument goes, were established by the privileged sectors of the population that have well-paid jobs, against those who merely want to accept the jobs they are offered.

Back in 1944, Hayek wrote in *The Road to Serfdom*:

> Never has a class been so cruelly exploited as are the weakest sectors of the working class by their privileged brothers—a form of exploitation made possible by the "regulation" of competition. Few slogans have done as much damage as the "stabilization" of prices and wages. By ensuring the wages of the few, the situation of the many is made increasingly precarious.[38]

To all intents and purposes, the World Bank said the same thing fifty years later in its 1995 report entitled "Workers in an Integrating World." Here are a few excerpts (author's emphasis):

> Through the obstacles it places to job creation, overly restrictive job-security regulations threaten to protect those in salaried positions **at the expense of excluded sectors, the unemployed and workers in the informal and rural sectors.**[39]

Down with job security! It thrives at the expense of the oppressed!

> There is good reason to fear that those who most benefit from social security—usually well-off workers—do so **at the expense of other workers.**[40]

Down with social security!

> There can be no doubt that trade unions often behave like monopolies to secure improvements in wages and working conditions for their members **at the expense of** holders of capital, consumers and **the non-unionized work force.**[41]

Down with the trade unions!

Hayek and Friedman have imitators in the East. Václav Klaus, elected president of the Czech Republic in 2003, told the British weekly *The Economist*:

The Western European social system is too much a prisoner of rules and excessive controls. The Welfare State, with all its generous transfer payments unconditioned by criteria relating to the efforts and merits of the people concerned, destroys the work ethic and feelings of individual responsibility. Public-sector workers are too protected. The Thatcher revolution—that is, the liberal, anti-Keynesian revolution—is in midstream in Western Europe. It has to be taken to the other shore.[43]

The World Bank Report "Doing Business": A Summary of Neoliberal Policy

IN 2009, at the height of a global crisis that sent the number of unemployed shooting skywards, the World Bank continued to advocate the elimination of social protection for workers. In its report "Doing Business 2010,"[44] its largest circulation annual review published in September 2009, the Bank explains its strategy for fighting the informal economy by emphasising that "states with more flexible employment regulations saw a 25% larger decrease in informal firms."

Since its first report "Doing Business 2003," the World Bank has annually classified the countries making the most reforms designed to improve the "business climate." The objective is to constantly reinforce the rights of investors and private property to the detriment of social rights. In fact, to establish its ranking of most "developed" economies, the World Bank uses an indicator relating to the hiring and firing of workers. The more a country's legislation facilitates firing, the better it places in the ranking. In spite of the many criticisms from social movements and the International Trade Union Confederation, the World Bank still persists in urging countries to lower severance pay and reduce or remove obligations regarding notice of termination.

By way of example, Rwanda in 2009 showed the greatest progress—and for good reason: employers are no longer obliged to organize prior consultation with employees' representatives (concerning reorganization) or to give notice to the labor inspectorate. On the other hand, Portugal has gone down in the ranking for extending the notice of termination period by two weeks. The list of countries downgraded for (slightly) improving workers' conditions is a long one. This doesn't stop the World Bank from affirming with extraordinary confidence that "the *Doing Business* employing workers indicators are fully consistent with the core labor standards but do not measure compliance with them." However, Belarus, which has been stripped of EU trade preferences for having violated fundamental conventions of the International Labor Organization (ILO) scored high in "Doing Business 2010." Going up in the "Doing Business" classification is therefore not good news for a country's population because it is a sign of social regression.

Finally, it should be noted that the bank is logically satisfied with the record-breaking number of antisocial reforms implemented this year, and congratulates Eastern Europe, "particularly active this year."[45] In fact, since 2008 some fifteen countries in this region have signed agreements with the IMF. And the World Bank certainly intends to encourage a new offensive of capital against labor under the pretext of the global crisis. Despite its highly publicized efforts to turn a new page under the direction of the socialist Dominique Strauss-Kahn, the IMF also continues to advocate antisocial policies in both North and South. In June 2009, à propos of the euro zone, the IMF declared that "the measures taken to support shorter working hours and raise social benefits—while important to shore up incomes and keep the labor force attached to the labor market—should have built-in reversibility."[46]

In another document drawn up especially by the World Bank for the Global Summit on Social Development, organized by the UN in Copenhagen in March 1995, the bank says that for Third World countries: "Minimum wages, unemployment insurance, redundancy payments and job-security legislation are of no use to rural and informal workers, who account for the majority of the poor in developing countries."[47]

This type of statement is in perfect harmony with those made by another champion of neoconservatism, Gilder, for whom: "Social security now erodes both work and the family, keeping the poor in poverty."[48] It is worth pointing out that Gilder favors such an approach for the entire planet, including the industrialized countries! Such declarations are reminiscent of something Thomas Robert Malthus said: "To be sure, the Poor Laws can be seen as weakening the willingness and ability of the common people for uplift. In this way, they weaken one of the most powerful motives for work."[49]

Alan Greenspan falls in line behind Malthus, Gilder, Hayek, and the World Bank when he writes, "Social safety nets exist virtually everywhere, to a greater or lesser extent. By their nature, they inhibit the full exercise of laissez-faire, mainly through labor laws and income redistribution programs."[50]

Furthermore, Greenspan cannot see why there should be legally fixed limits on CEOs' wages, "Even given the flawed aspects of corporate governance, executive salaries are ultimately and, one must assume, voluntarily assented to by the company's shareholders. As I noted earlier, there should be no role for government in this transaction. Wage control, like price control, invariably leads to grave unexpected distortions."

He adds the icing to the neoliberal cake in stating, "The autocratic-CEO paradigm appears to be the only arrangement that allows for the effective functioning of a corporation. We cannot get around the authoritarian imperative of today's corporate structure."[51]

The visionary capacity of this great neoliberal Alan Greenspan must be emphasized. Just before the financial system, which he had helped deregulate, started to collapse in 2007–08, Greenspan wrote: "In order to facilitate the financing, insuring, and timeliness of all that trade, the volume of cross-border transactions in financial instruments has had to rise even faster than the trade itself. Wholly new forms of finance had to be invented or developed—credit derivatives, asset-backed securities, oil futures, and the like all make the world's trading system function far more efficiently." Finally, Greenspan states that the economy had found a rhythm of continual growth and great stability thanks to the invisible hand, "In many respects, the apparent stability of our global trade and financial system is a reaffirmation of the simple, time-tested principle promulgated by Adam Smith in 1776: Individuals trading freely with one another following their own self-interest leads to a growing, stable economy."[52]

What is the bank of Sweden waiting for to award him the Nobel Prize in economics?[53]

Globalization from Christopher Columbus and Vasco da Gama until Today[1]

First part
March 2008

THE BEGINNING of globalization goes back to the outcomes of the first voyage of Christopher Columbus that brought him, in October 1492, to the shore of an island in the Caribbean Sea. It was the starting point of a brutal and bloody intervention of European sea powers in the history of American peoples, a region of the world that had, up to then, remained insulated from regular relationships with Europe, Africa, and Asia. The Spanish conquistadors and their Portuguese, British, French, and Dutch[2] counterparts together conquered the whole geographical area, commonly known as the Americas,[3] by causing the death of the vast majority of the indigenous population in order to exploit the natural resources (in particular gold and silver).[4] Simultaneously, European powers started the conquest of Asia. Later on, they completed their domination in Australia and finally Africa.

In 1500, just at the beginning of the brutal intervention of the Spaniards and the Portuguese in Central and South America, this region had at least eighteen million inhabitants (some authors put forward much larger figures of close to a hundred million[5]). One century later, only around eight million inhabitants were left (including European settlers and the first African slaves). In the case of most islands of the Caribbean Sea, the whole indigenous population had been wiped out. It is worth recalling that during a long period of time, Europeans, supported by the Vatican,[6] did not consider indigenous people from the Americas as human beings.[7] A convenient justification for exploitation and extermination.

Table 1. Comparison between evolution of the population in Western Europe and Latin America between 1500 and 1820 (in millions).

	1500	1600	1700	1820
Western Europe	57	74	81	133
Latin America	18	8 *	12 *	21

*Those two figures include indigenous people from the Americas, European settlers, and slaves brought by force from Africa. Calculations of Eric Toussaint based upon Angus Madison, 2001.

In North America, the European colonization started during the seventeenth century, mainly led by England and France, before undergoing a rapid expansion during the eighteenth century, an era also marked by massive importation of African slaves. Indigenous populations were either wiped out or driven outside the settlement zones of European settlers. In 1700, the indigenous population constituted three-quarters of the population; in 1820, their proportion had dropped down to 3 percent.

Until the forced integration of the Americas in global commerce, the main axis of intercontinental trade exchanges involved China, India, and Europe.[8] Trade between Europe and China followed terrestrial and maritime routes (via the Black Sea).[9] The main route linking Europe to India (whether from the state of Gujarat in Northwest India, or from Kerala and the Calicut or Cochin harbors in the Southwest) passed through the Mediterranean Sea, Alexandria, Syria, the Arabian Peninsula, and finally the Arabian Sea. India also played an active role in trade exchanges between China and Europe.

Until the fifteenth century, technical progress achieved in Europe relied upon technology transfers from Asia and the Arab world.

At the end of the fifteenth century and during the sixteenth century, trade started to follow other routes. When the Genoese, Christopher

Columbus, serving under the Spanish crown, opened the maritime route towards the "Americas"[10] by sailing west through the Atlantic, the Portuguese sailor, Vasco da Gama, made for India, also through the Atlantic but heading south. He sailed along the Western coasts of Africa from north to south, veering east after crossing the Cape of Good Hope in the south of Africa.[11] Violence, coercion, and robbery were central to the methods employed by Christopher Columbus and Vasco da Gama to serve the interests of the Spanish and Portuguese crowns. During the following centuries, European powers and their servants would systematically use terror, extermination, and extortion, combined with the search for compliant local allies. Several peoples worldwide would witness the brutal deviation of their history's course under the whips of the conquistadors, settlers, and European capital. Other peoples would suffer from an even more terrible fate since they were wiped out or reduced to the situation of foreigners in their own countries. Still others were uprooted by force from one continent to another to serve as slaves.

Admittedly, prior to the fifteenth century of the Christian era, history had been marked on several occasions by conquests, dominations, and barbarity without however touching the whole planet. What is striking of the last five centuries is that European powers started conquering the whole world and, within three centuries, interlinked (almost) all peoples of the world through brutal ways. During the same time, the capitalist logic finally succeeded in dominating all other modes of production (without necessarily eliminating them entirely).

At the end of the fifteenth century, capitalist commercialization of the world received a first boost, subsequently followed by others, namely the nineteenth-century diffusion of the industrial revolution from Western Europe and the "late" colonization of Africa by the European powers. The first international economic crisis (in industry, finance, and trade) exploded at the beginning of the nineteenth century, leading to the first debt crises.[12] The twentieth century has been the scene of two world wars, with Europe as their epicenter, and unsuccessful attempts to implement socialism. In the seventies, the turn of global capitalism towards neoliberalism, and the restoration of capitalism in the former Soviet Bloc and China have provided a new boost to globalization.

Second Intercontinental Voyage of Vasco da Gama (1502): Lisbon—Cape of Good Hope—Eastern Africa—India (Kerala)

AFTER A first successful voyage to India in 1497–99, Vasco da Gama was again assigned by the Portuguese crown to return there with a fleet of twenty ships. He left Lisbon in February 1502. Fifteen ships would have to come back while five (under the command of da Gama's uncle) would stay behind, both to protect Portuguese bases in India and to block ships leaving towards the Red Sea, thus shutting off trade between the two areas. Da Gama rounded the Cape in June, stopping in Sofala, East Africa, to buy gold.[13] In Kilwa, he forced the local sovereign to make an annual payment of pearls and gold before making for India. Off Cannanore (seventy kilometers north of Calicut—today Kozhikode), da Gama waited for Arab ships returning from the Red Sea to seize a ship on route from Mecca with pilgrims and a valuable cargo. Part of the cargo was seized and the ship set on fire, resulting in the death of most of its passengers and crew. Next stop was Cannanore where he swapped gifts (gold for precious stones) with the local sovereign without making business, estimating that the price of spices were too high. He sailed for Cochin (today Kochi), stopped his ships in front of Calicut, and asked the sovereign to expel the whole Muslim trading community (4,000 households) who used the harbor as a base for commerce with the Red Sea.

Following the Samudri's (local Hindu sovereign) refusal, Vasco da Gama ordered the bombardment of the town, following in the footsteps of another Portuguese sailor, Pedro Cabal, in 1500. He set out for Cochin at the beginning of November where he bought spices in exchange for silver, copper, and textiles stolen from the sunken ship. A permanent trading post was established in Cochin and five ships were left there to protect Portuguese interests.

Before leaving India for Portugal, da Gama's fleet was attacked by more than thirty ships financed by Calicut Muslim traders. A Portuguese bombardment led to their defeat. Consequently, a part of Calicut's Muslim trading community decided to base their operations elsewhere. Those naval battles clearly demonstrate the violence and criminal nature of the action of Vasco da Gama and the Portuguese fleet.

Da Gama returned to Lisbon in October 1503 with thirteen of his ships and approximately 1,700 tons of spices, that is, around the same amount imported from the Middle East at the end of the fifteenth century by Venice. Portuguese profit margins from this trade were much larger than those of Venetians. A major part of the spices was sold in

Europe via Antwerp, the major harbor of the Spanish Netherlands, then the most important European harbor.

Maritime Chinese Expeditions During the Fifteenth Century

EUROPEANS WERE not the only ones traveling far away and discovering new maritime routes. But they were the most aggressive and the most conquering.

Several decades before Vasco da Gama, between 1405 and 1433, seven Chinese expeditions headed west and notably visited Indonesia, Malaysia, India, Sri Lanka, the Arabian peninsula (the Strait of Hormuz and the Red Sea), and the eastern coast of Africa (notably Mogadishu and Malindi).

Under Emperor Yongle, the Ming marine "included approximately a total of 3,800 ships, among which were 1,350 patrol boats and 1,350 battle ships incorporated into defense or insular bases, a main fleet of 400 heavy battleships stationed near Nanking, and 400 loading ships for cereal transportation. Moreover, there were more than twenty treasure-boats, ships equipped to undertake large-scale action.[14] They were five times larger than any ship of da Gama, 120 meters long and nearly 50 meters wide. The large boats possessed fifteen watertight compartments so that a damaged ship would not sink and could be repaired at sea.

Their intentions were pacifist but their military force was sufficiently imposing to fend off attacks that only took place three times. The first expedition aimed towards India and its spices. Others were geared towards exploring the eastern coast of Africa, the Red Sea, and the Persian Gulf.

The main goal of these voyages was to establish good relationships by offering gifts and escorting ambassadors or sovereigns that were coming to or leaving China. No attempt was ever made to establish bases for trade or military purposes. The Chinese were looking for new plants for medicinal needs and one of the missions comprised 180 members of the medical profession. In contrast, during the first voyage of Vasco da Gama to India, his crew included approximately 160 men, among whom were gunners, musicians, and three Arab interpreters. After 1433, the Chinese abandoned their lengthy maritime expeditions and gave priority to internal development.

In 1500, Standards of Living Were Comparable

WHEN, AT the end of the fifteenth century, Western European powers launched their conquests of the rest of the world, European standards of living and level of development were no higher than those of other large areas of the world. China was unquestionably ahead of Western Europe in many ways: in people's living conditions, in the sciences, infrastructure,[15] and agricultural and manufacturing processes. India was more or less on a par with Europe, as far as living conditions and quality of manufactured goods were concerned (Indian textiles and iron were of better quality than European products).[16] The Inca civilization in the Andes in Southern America and the Aztecs in Mexico were also flourishing and very advanced. We should be cautious when defining criteria for measuring development and avoid limiting ourselves to the calculation of GDP per capita. Having said that, even if we take this measure and add life expectancy and quality of food available, the Europeans did not live any better than the inhabitants of other large areas of the world prior to their conquering expeditions.

Intra-Asian Trade before the European Powers Burst onto the Scene

IN 1500 Asia's population was five times that of Western Europe. The Indian population alone was twice that of Western Europe.[17] Hence, it represented a very large market, with a network of Asian traders operating between East Africa and Western India, and between Eastern India and Indonesia. East of the Malacca Straits, trade was dominated by China.

Asian traders knew the seasonal wind patterns and navigation hazards of the Indian Ocean well. There were many experienced sailors in the area, and they had a wealth of scientific literature available on astronomy and navigation. Their navigation tools left them with little to envy those of the Portuguese.

From East Africa to Malacca (in the narrow straits separating Sumatra from Malaysia), Asian trade was conducted by communities of merchants who did their business without armed gunships nor heavy government intervention. Things changed radically with the methods used by the Portuguese, Dutch, English, and French, serving state and merchant interests. The maritime expeditions launched by the European powers to various parts of Asia increased considerably, as shown in the table below (from Maddison, 2001). It shows clearly that Portugal was the indisputable European power in Asia in the sixteenth century. The following century it was replaced by the Dutch, who remained dominant throughout the eighteenth century, and the English were in second place.

Table 2. Number of ships sent to Asia by seven European countries, 1500-1800

Country	1500-1599	1600-1700	1701-1800
Portugal	705	371	196
Netherlands	65*	1770	2950
England		811	1865
France		155	1300
Other countries		54	350
Total	770	3161	6661

*in the 1590s

Sources: Portugal 1500-1800, data from Magalhaes Godinho in Bruijn Gaastra (1993) pp. 7 and 17; other data from Bruijn and Gaastra (1993), pp 178 and 183. The 'other countries' include Danish and Swedish merchant ships and those of the Ostend Company.

Great Britain joins the Other European Powers in the Conquest of the World

IN THE sixteenth century, England's main occupations outside Europe were piracy and reconnaissance trips to explore the possibility of setting up a colonial empire. The most daring act was the royal support given to Drake's (1577–80) expedition which, with five ships and 116 crew, rounded the Strait of Magellan, captured and plundered the treasure-laden Spanish ships off the Chilean and Peruvian coasts, set up useful contacts with the spice islands of the Molucca Sea, Java, Cape of Good Hope, and Guinea on the way home.[18] At the end of the sixteenth century, Great Britain scored the decisive victory which sealed its status as a naval power when it defeated the Spanish Armada off the British coast.

From that moment on, Britain plunged into the conquest of the New World and Asia. In the New World it set up sugar-producing colonies in the Carribean and, from the 1620s on, was an active participant in the trading of slaves imported from Africa. Simultaneously, between 1607 and 1713 it set up fifteen colonies of settlement in North America, thirteen of which ended up declaring their independence and becoming, in 1776, the United States, while the other two stayed within the British circle and were to become part of Canada.

In Asia, the British crown adopted a different policy: rather than settler colonies, it set up a system of exploitation colonies, starting with India. To this end, the British state granted its protection to the East India Company (an association of merchants in competition with other similar groups in Great Britain) in 1600. In 1702 the state bestowed a trade monopoly on the East India Company and threw itself into the fight for the subcontinent, which ended with the British victory at the Battle of Plassey in 1757, giving them control of Bengal. For a little over two centuries, Great Britain applied an uncompromising protectionist economic policy, and once it had become the dominant economic power during the nineteenth century, it imposed an imperialist free-trade policy. For example, with the help of gunboats, it imposed "free trade" on China, forcing the latter to buy Indian opium while allowing the British to buy Chinese tea for resale on the European market with the proceeds of the opium sales.

Elsewhere, Britain extended its conquests in Asia (Burma, Malaysia), in Australasia (Australia, New Zealand, etc.), in North Africa (Egypt), and in the Near East. As for sub-Saharan Africa, until the nineteenth century, its only major interest was the slave trade. Later on, the conquest of Africa became an objective.

Goa: A Portuguese Enclave in India

In India, as in other parts of Asia, the English had been preceded by the Portuguese, who conquered small parcels of Indian territory. They set up trading posts and installed religious terrorism. As such, an Inquisition court was set up in Goa in 1560, which imposed its cruelty until 1812. In 1567, all Hindu ceremonies were banned. In just over two centuries, sixteen thousand sentences were pronounced by the Goa Inquisition and thousands of Indians were burned at the stake.

The British Conquest of the Indies

The British, in their conquest of India, expelled their other European rivals, the Dutch and the French. The latter were determined to prevail, but they could not do so. Their defeat in the Seven Years War against the British was mainly due to insufficient support from the French state.[19]

To take control of India, the British systematically sought out allies amongst the local rulers and ruling classes. They did not hesitate to use force, when deemed necessary, as in the Battle of Plassey in 1757 and the violent repression of the Sepoy Rebellion in 1859. They bent the local power structures to their service and generally left the local lords in place, allowing them to continue to lead an ostentatious life, although the rules of the game were dictated by others (they were powerless against the British). The division of society into castes was maintained and even reinforced, which still weighs heavily on today's India. In effect, the division of society into classes and gender domination were reinforced by a division into castes, based on birth. Through taxation and unfair terms of trade between India and Great Britain, the Indian people contributed to the enrichment of Britain both as a country and in terms of its rich classes (merchants, industrialists, and politicians). But the British are not the only ones who got rich: bankers, merchants, and Indian manufacturers also accumulated immense fortunes. Thanks to them, the East India Company and the British state managed to exert, for such a long time, a domination which the people profoundly rejected.

The Example of the Cotton Industry

The quality of textiles and cotton produced in India was unrivalled anywhere in the world. The British tried to copy the Indian production techniques and produce cotton of comparable quality at home, but for a long time the results were quite poor. Under pressure, particularly from the owners of British cotton mills, the British government prohibited the export of Indian cotton to any part of the British Empire. London further forbade the East India Company to trade Indian cotton outside the empire, thus closing all possible outlets for Indian textiles. Only thanks to these measures was Britain able to make its own cotton industry really profitable.

Today, while the British and other industrialized powers systematically apply the Intellectual Property Rights Treaty (Trade Related Aspects of Intellectual Property Rights—TRIPs) within the World Trade Organization, to demand payments from developing countries such as India, less than three centuries ago they had no qualms about copying Indian production methods and design, specifically in the textiles field.[20]

Furthermore, to increase their profits and become more competitive than the Indian cotton industry, the British owners of cotton companies decided to introduce new production techniques: steam-powered machinery and new looms and spinning machines. Through the use of force, the British fundamentally changed India's development. Whereas up to the end of the eighteenth century, the Indian economy exported high quality manufactured goods and could satisfy most domestic demands, in the nineteenth and twentieth centuries it was invaded by European products, particularly from Britain. Great Britain prevented India from exporting its manufactured goods, forced it to export increasing quantities of opium to China in the nineteenth century (just as it coerced China to buy the opium) and flooded the Indian market with British manufactures. In short, it produced underdevelopment in India.

In the second part of this article we will discuss colonial famines, triangulation, the World Bank, IMF, and WTO interventions compared to the current Indian miracle, and explore some alternative paths.

Translation from French: Jean-Pierre Schermann and Lorraine Buckley, Coorditrad. Revised by Diren Valayden.

The Market:
The New Faith

PRACTICALLY ALL political leaders—whether from the traditional Left or the Right, from the North or the South—have a quasi-religious faith in the market, especially the financial markets. Or rather, they themselves are the high priests of this religion. Every day in every country, anyone with a television or an Internet connection can attend mass and worship the market-god—in the form of stock exchange and financial market reports. The market-god sends his messages through television anchormen and the financial editors of daily newspapers. Today, this happens not only in Organization for Economic Cooperation and Development (OECD) countries, but in most parts of the planet. Whether you are in Shangai or Dakar, Rio de Janeiro or Timbuktu, you can receive "market signals." Everywhere, governments have privatized and created the illusion that the population will be able to participate directly in market rituals (by buying shares) and reap the benefits in accordance with how well one interprets signals sent by the market-god. In actual fact, the small part of the working population that has acquired shares has no say over market tendencies.

In a few centuries, the history books might say that from the 1980s onwards a fetishist cult prospered. The dramatic rise of this cult will perhaps be associated with two heads of state, Margaret Thatcher and Ronald Reagan. It will be noted that, from the start, this cult had the backing of governments and powerful private financial interests. Indeed, for this cult to gain ground within the population, public and private media found it necessary to pay homage to it day in and day out.

The gods of this religion are the financial markets. Its temples are known as stock exchanges. Only the high priests and their acolytes can tread their holy ground. The faithful are called upon to commune with their market-god on television, on their computer screen, in the daily papers, on the radio or at the bank. Thanks to television, radio, and the Internet even in the most remote parts of the planet, hundreds of millions of people who are deprived of the right to meet their basic needs, are also urged to celebrate the market-god. In the North, in newspapers read by a majority of workers, housewives, and unemployed, an "investment" section is published every day, even though the overwhelming majority of readers do not own a single share. Journalists are paid to help the faithful understand signals sent by the gods.

To heighten the power of the gods in the eyes of the faithful, commentators periodically declare that the gods have sent signals to governments to express their satisfaction or discontent. The Greek government and parliament have at last understood the message sent by the gods and adopted a drastic austerity plan that has the lower classes paying the price. But the gods are dissatisfied with Spain, Portugal, Italy, and Ireland. Their governments too will have to contribute their ritual offerings in the guise of strong antisocial measures.

The places where the gods are most likely to forcefully express their moods are Wall Street in New York, the City in London, and the Paris, Frankfurt, and Tokyo stock exchanges. To gauge their moods, special indicators have been devised: the Dow Jones in New York, the Nikkei in Tokyo, the CAC40 in France, the Footsie in London, the Dax in Francfort. To appease the gods, governments must sacrifice the welfare state to the stock markets. They must also privatize public property.

Why are ordinary market operators given a religious aura? They are neither anonymous nor ethereal. They have names, addresses. They are the people in charge of the 200 biggest Trade Negotiation Committees (TNCs) that control the world with the help of the G7, the G20, and institutions such as the IMF, which came back into the limelight thanks to the financial crisis. Next we also have the World Bank and the World Trade Organization, currently in a rather difficult predicament, but who knows, the gods might favour it again soon. Governments are no strangers to this situation; from Reagan and Thatcher onwards, they relinquished the means they had of controlling financial markets. The situation is now almost reversed: institutional investors (i.e. major banks, pension funds, insurance companies, hedge funds, etc.) received trillions of dollars from governments in the form of grants or loans to bail them out after the 2007–08 meltdown. The European Central Bank, the US Federal Reserve, and the Bank of England now lend them money on a daily basis at a lower rate than the capital inflation that institutional investors immediately use to speculate against the euro and against public money.

Money can cross borders without a single cent in taxes being levied. More than $3 trillion race around the planet every day. Less than 2 percent of this amount is linked to actual trade in goods and services or to productive investments. More than 98 percent is used for purely speculative operations mainly on currencies, on commodities, and on debt securities.

We have to put a stop to this death-breeding logic. We have to develop a new financial discipline, to expropriate the financial sector, and exert social democratic control on all financial matters, to tax all institutional investors (which triggered and then profited from the crisis) heavily, to audit and cancel public debts, to implement a distributive tax reform, to drastically reduce working hours so as to offer more jobs while maintaining wages at their current level... In short, we must launch an anticapitalist project.

Translated by Raghu Krishnan in collaboration with Vicki Briault, Christine Pagnoulle, and Judith Harris.

The Irish Crisis:
A Complete Failure
for Neoliberalism[1]

FOR A decade, Ireland was heralded by the most ardent partisans of neoliberal capitalism as a model to be imitated. The Celtic Tiger had a higher growth rate than the European average. Tax rates on companies had been reduced to 12.5 percent[2] and the rate actually paid by TNCs that had set up business there was between 3 and 4 percent—a CEO's dream! Ireland's budget deficit was nil in 2007, as was its unemployment rate in 2008. In this earthly paradise, everybody seemed to benefit. Workers had jobs (though often highly precarious), their families were busy consuming, benefiting as they were from the prevailing abundance, and both local and foreign capitalists were enjoying inordinate returns.

In October 2008, a couple of days before the Belgian government bailed out the big "Belgian" banks Fortis and Dexia with taxpayers' money, Bruno Colmant, head of the Brussels stock exchange and professor of economics, published an op-ed in *Le Soir*, the French-language daily newspaper of record, stating that Belgium imperatively had to follow the Irish example and further deregulate its financial system. According to Colmant, Belgium needed to change the legal and institutional framework so as to become a platform for international capital, just like Ireland. A few short weeks later the Celtic Tiger was crying mercy.

In Ireland, financial deregulation had triggered a boom in loans to households (household indebtedness had reached 190 percent of GDP on the eve of the crisis), particularly in real estate, a factor that helped boost the island's economy (the building industry, financial activities, etc.). The banking sector had experienced exponential growth with the establishment of many foreign companies[3] and the increase in Irish banks' assets. Real estate and stock market bubbles started forming. The total amount of stock market capitalizations, bond issues, and bank assets was fourteen times bigger than the country's GDP.

What could not possibly happen in such a fairy tale world then happened: in September–October 2008 the card castle collapsed and the real estate and financial bubbles burst. Companies closed down or left the country, unemployment rose from 0 percent in 2008 to 14 percent in early 2010. The number of families unable to repay their creditors swiftly increased too. The whole Irish banking system teetered on the edge of bankruptcy and a panic-stricken government blindly guaranteed bank deposits for EU480 billion (that is, about three times an Irish GDP of 168 billion). It nationalized the Allied Irish Bank, the main source of financing for real estate loans, with a transfusion of EU48.5 billion (about 30 percent of GDP).

Exports slowed down. State revenues declined. The budget deficit rose from 14 percent of GDP in 2009 to 32 percent in 2010 (more than half of this due to the massive support given to the banks: 46 billion in equity and 31 billion in purchases of toxic assets).

At the end of 2010 the European bailout plan with IMF participation amounted to EU85 billion in loans (including $22.5 billion from the IMF) and it is already clear that it will not be enough. In exchange, a radical cure was enforced upon the Celtic Tiger in the form of a drastic austerity plan that heavily affects households' purchasing power, with a resultant decrease in consumption, in public expenditure on welfare, in civil servants' salaries, in infrastructure investments (to facilitate debt repayment), and in tax revenues. On the social level, the principal measures of the austerity plan are nothing short of disastrous:

- Suppression of 24,750 positions in the civil service (8 percent of the workforce, which would mean 350,000 positions in France);
- Newly recruited employees will earn 10 percent less;
- Reduction of social transfers resulting in lower family and unemployment allowances, a significant reduction in the health budget, a freeze on retirement pensions;
- A rise in taxes, to be borne mostly by the majority of the population, already victims of the crisis: notably a VAT increase from 21 percent to 23 percent in 2014; creation of a real estate tax (affect-

ing half of the households that were formerly tax-exempt);
- A EU1 reduction in the minimum hourly wage (from EU8.65 to 7.65, or 11 percent less).

The rates for loans to Ireland are very high: 5.7 percent for the IMF loan and 6.05 percent for "EU" loans. These loans will be used to repay banks and other financial bodies that buy bonds on the Irish debt, borrowing money from the European Central Bank at a rate of 1 percent—another windfall for private financiers. According to Agence France-Presse, IMF managing director Dominique Strauss-Kahn claimed that it would work, though of course "it would be difficult because it is hard for people who will have to make sacrifices for the sake of budget austerity."

Both in the streets and in parliament, opposition has been very determined. The Dail, or lower house of parliament, voted the EU85 billion rescue plan by a mere eighty-one to seventy-five. Far from relinquishing its neoliberal orientation, the IMF declared that among Ireland's priorities it is counting on the adoption of reforms to do away with structural obstacles to business, so as to support competitiveness in the coming years. "Socialist" Dominique Strauss-Kahn said he was convinced that a new government after the elections in early 2011 would not change anything: *"I'm confident that even if the opposition parties, Fine Gael and Labor, are criticizing the government and the programme [. . .], they understand the need to implement the programme."*

In short, the economic and financial liberalization aimed at attracting foreign investments and transnational financial companies has utterly failed. To add insult to the damage the population must bear as a result of such a policy, the IMF and the Irish government are persevering in the neoliberal orientation of the past two decades and, under pressure from international finance, are subjecting the population to a structural adjustment programme similar to those imposed on Third World countries for the past three decades. Yet these decades should show what must not be done, and why it is high time to enforce a radically different logic that benefits people and not private money.

Translated by Christine Pagnoulle in collaboration with Judith Harris.

Bibliography*

* Year in brackets indicates the date of the first edition

Adda, Jacques. *La mondialisation de l'économie.* Paris: La Découverte, 1996.

Amin, Samir. *L'accumulation à l'échelle mondiale : Critique de la théorie du sous-développement.* Paris: Anthropos, 1971 [1970].

————. *Mondialisation et accumulation.* Paris: L'Harmattan, 1993.

Anderson, Perry. "Histoire et leçons du néo-libéralisme: La construction d'une voie unique." *Page Deux* (October 1996).

Bairoch, Paul. (1993). *Mythes et paradoxes de l'histoire économique.* Paris: La Découverte/Poche, 1999, 288

Baran, Paul A. and Paul M. Sweezy. *Le capitalisme monopoliste,* Paris: François Maspero, 1970 [1966].

Bayly, Christopher Alan. (2004). *La naissance du monde moderne (1780–1914).* Paris: Les Editions de l'Atelier/Editions Ouvrières, 2007.

Beaud, Michel and Gilles Dostaler. *La pensée économique depuis Keynes.* Paris: Seuil, 1996 [1993].

Becker, Gary. *The Economic Approach to Human Approach.* Chicago: University of Chicago Press, 1976.

Bensaïd, Daniel. *Marx l'intempestif.* Paris: Fayard, 1995.

Braudel, Fernand. *Civilisation and Capitalism, 15th–18th Century,* 3 vol. Londres: Fontana, 1985.

Cardoso, Fernando Henrique and Enzo Faletto. *Dependencia y desarrollo en América latina.* Mexico: Siglo XXI, 1970 [1969].

Chaudhuri, K.N. *The Trading World of Asia and the English East India Company, 1660–1760.* Cambridge: Cambridge University Press, 1978.

Chaudhury, Sushil. *From Prosperity to Decline: Eighteenth Century Bengal,* New Delhi: Manohar, 1999.

Chaudhury, Sushil and Michel Morineau. *Merchants, Companies and Trade: Europe and Asia in the Early Modern Era,* Cambridge: Cambridge University Press, 1999.

Chesnais, François. *La mondialisation du capital.* Paris: Syros, 1994.

———, ed. *La mondialisation financière : genèse, coûts et enjeux.* Paris : Syros, 1996.

———. *La mondialisation du capital.* 2d ed. Paris: Syros, 1997.

Chesnais, François, Gérard Duménil, Dominique Lévy, and Immanuel Wallerstein. *Une nouvelle phase du capitalisme.* Paris: Syllepse, 2001.

Clairmont, Frederic F. *The Rise and Fall of Economic Liberalism.* Malaysia: Southbound and Third World Network, 356. 1996.

Colomb, Cristophe. *La découverte de l'Amérique I. Journal de bord. 1492-1493,* Paris: François Maspero, La Découverte. 1980, 235.

———. *La découverte de l'Amérique II. Journal de bord. 1493-1504,* Paris: François Maspero, La Découverte. 1980, 225 .

Davis, Mike. *Late Victorian Holocausts, El Nino Famines and the Making of the Third World.* London: Verso, 2001.

Dewey, John. "The Future of Liberalism," *The Journal of Philosophy,* XXII, no. 9 (1935): 225–30.

Dos Santos, Theotonio. *Imperialismo y dependencia.* Mexico: Era, 1982 [1978].

Friedman, Milton. *The Counter-Revolution in Monetary Theory.* London: Institute of Economic Affairs, 1970.

Galbraith, John Kenneth. *La crise économique de 1929: Anatomie d'une catastrophe financière.* Paris: Payot, 2008 [1954].

Gilder, George. *Richesse et pauvreté.* Paris : Albin Michel, 1981.

Greenspan, Alan. *The Age of Turbulence: Adventures in a New World.* New York: Penguin Press, 2007.

Gunder Frank, André. *Lumpen-bourgeoisie et lumpen-développement.* Paris: Maspero, 1971.

———. *L'Accumulation mondiale, 1500–1800.* Paris: Calmann-Lévy, 1977.

Hayek von, Friedrich August. *The Road to Serfdom.* London: Routledge Press, 1944.

Keynes, John. M. *The General Theory of Employment Interest and Money.* London: MacMillan, 1964 [1936].

Labica, Georges and Gérard Bensussan. *Dictionnaire critique du marxisme.* Paris: P.U.F, 1982.

Luxemburg, Rosa. *L'accumulation du capital,* tome II. Paris: François Maspero, 1967, 238. 1913.

Maddison, Angus. *L'économie mondiale : une perspective millénaire,* Centre de Développement de l'Organisation de coopération et de développement économiques (OCDE), Paris, 2001, 403. 2001.

Malthus, Thomas Robert. *An Essay on the Principle of Population*. J. Johnson, 1798.

Mandel, Ernest. *Late Capitalism*. London: NLB, 1975, 599.

———. *Long Waves of Capitalist Development: A Marxist Interpretation*. Cambridge/Paris: Cambridge University Press/Editions de la Maison des Sciences de l'Homme, 1980 (based on the Marshall Lectures given at the University of Cambridge in 1978).

Marini, Ruy Mauro. *Dialéctica de la dependencia*. Mexico: Era, 1973.

Marx, Karl. *Le Capital, livre I, Œuvres I*. La Pléiade: Gallimard, 1963, 1818.

———. *Capital*. 3 vol. London: Penguin Classics, 1993 [1867, 1885, 1894].

———. *Fondements de la critique de l'économie politique. Ebauche de 1857–1858 (Grundrisse der Kritik der politischen Ökonomie)*. 6 vol. Paris: 10/18, 1972.

———. *Critique des programmes de Gotha et d'Erfurt*. Paris: Les Editions Sociales, 1966.

Marx, Karl and Friedrich Engels. *La Crise*. Paris: Union générale d'éditions, 1978.

Millet, Damien and Eric Toussaint. *La crise, quelles crises?* Brussels/Liège/Geneva: Aden/CADTM/CETIM, 2010.

Needham, Joseph *et al. Science and Civilisation in China*. Cambridge: Cambridge University Press, 1954–2000.

Prebisch, Raúl. *Capitalismo periférico, crisis y transformación*. Mexico: Fondo de Cultura Económica, 1984 [1981].

Polo, Marco. *Le devisement du monde: Le livre des merveilles I*. Paris: François Maspero La Découverte, 1980.

Pomeranz, Kenneth. *The Great Divergence*. Princeton: Princeton University Press, 2000.

Ricardo, David. *On the Principles of Political Economy and Taxation*. London: Cambridge University Press, 1950 [1817].

Sahagún, Fray Bernardino de. *Histoire générale des choses de la Nouvelle-Espagne*, Paris: François Maspero, 1981, 299.

Salama, Pierre and Jacques Valier. *Pauvreté et in égalités dans le tiers monde*. Paris: La Découverte, 1994.

Shiva, Vandana. *The Violence of the green revolution*. Malaysia: Third World Network, 1993, 264, 1991.

Smith, Adam. *An Inquiry into the Nature and Causes of the Wealth of Na-*

tions. 1776, http://www.adamsmith.org/smith/.

Stiglitz, Joseph E. *Globalization and Its Discontents.* New York: W. W. Norton & Company, 2002.

———. *Quand le capitalisme perd la tête.* Paris: Fayard, 2003.

Subrahmanyam, Sanjay. *The Career and Legend of Vasco da Gama.* Cambridge: Cambridge University Press, 1997.

Tobin, James. "A Proposal for International Monetary Reform." *The Eastern Economic Journal* (July–October 1978).

Tobin, James, Barry J. Eichengreen, and Charles Wyplosz. (1995) "Two Cases for Sand in the Wheels of International Finance," in "Policy Forum: Sand in the Wheels of International Finance." *The Economic Journal* (January 1995): 162–72.

Toussaint, Eric. *Your Money or Your Life.* Chicago: Haymarket Books, 2005.

———. *The World Bank: A Critical Primer.* London: Pluto Press, 2007.

Udry, Charles-André. "Los orígenes del neoliberalismo: F von Hayek : el apostol del neoliberalismo." *Desde los Cuatro Puntos,* no. 1 (1997).

Urriola, Rafael, ed. *La globalización de los desajustes.* Caracas: Nueva Sociedad, 1996.

Wallerstein, Immanuel. *Le capitalisme historique,* Paris: Editions La Découverte, 1996, 119, 1983.

World Bank. *World Development Report : Workers in an Integrating World.* Washington, 1995.

———. *Promouvoir le développement social. Contribution de la Banque mondiale au Sommet social.* Washington, 1995.

———. *Doing Business 2010.* Washington, 2009.

Zinn, Howard, ed. *New Deal Thought.* Indianapolis : Hackett Publishing Company, 2003 [1966].

Notes

Introduction

1. The economic and financial crisis broke out in the United States in 2007, namely in the area of housing and mortgage with the bursting of a speculative bubble. From the start it hit major institutions both in the United States and in Europe (the UK, Germany, France, Switzerland, etc.). Simultaneously in 2007 a severe food crisis set in, affecting mainly the populations in developing countries (between the end of 2006 and 2009 the number of starving people has risen from 850 million to one billion). From 2008 on this multidimensional capitalist crisis has become a global one.

2. Alan Greenspan, *The Age of Turbulence: Adventures in a New World* (New York: The Penguin Press, 2007), Chapter 13.

A Glance in the Rearview Mirror

1. Alan Greenspan tells in his autobiography that when he first read Adam Smith after the Second World War, interest in his theories was particularly low. He points out that "free trade" was almost a rude word and that the most prominent partisans of market capitalism were mavericks such as Ayn Rand and Milton Friedman. He adds that it was at the end of the 1960s, at the outset of his public career, that the pendulum of economic thinking swung back towards Adam Smith. In Greenspan, *The Age of Turbulence.*

2. See Eric Toussaint, *The World Bank : A Critical Primer* (London: Pluto Press, 2007), Chapter 11, "South Korea: The Miracle Unmasked."

3. This is referring to the liberal ideological trends experienced in the European continent and which clearly place themselves on the right-hand side of the political spectrum. In the United States

the use of the term liberal has an entirely different meaning. The liberals of the United States belong to the center-left or moderate right. One such liberal and progressive figure in the United States is John Dewey (1859–1952). In particular, see John Dewey, "The Future of Liberalism," *The Journal of Philosophy*, XXII, no. 9, 225–30 in Howard Zinn, ed., *New Deal Thought* (Indianapolis: Hackett Publishing Company, 2003).

4. Throughout the 1970s, the global economy entered a long phase of slow expansion which broke with the previous almost thirty years of unprecedented rapid economic growth, famously known as the "Glorious Thirty."

5. Adam Smith, *An Inquiry into the Nature And Causes of the Wealth of Nations*, 1776: Book IV, Chapter 2. http://www.adamsmith.org/smith/won-b4-c2.htm.

6. Smith, *Wealth of Nations*, Book IV, Chapter 2.

7. Smith, *Wealth of Nations*, Book V, Chapter 1, Part 3. http://www.adamsmith.org/smith/won-b5-c1-pt-3.htm.

8. Smith, *Wealth of Nations*, Book I, Chapter 5. http://www.adamsmith.org/smith/won-b1-c5.htm. Adam Smith further writes: "*Labor measures the value not only of that part of price which resolves itself into labor* (salary, editor's note), *but of that which resolves itself into rent, and of that which resolves itself into profit.*" (Smith, *Wealth of Nations*, Book I, Chapter 6. http://www.adamsmith.org/smith/won-b1-c6.htm). Alan Greenspan, who claims to adhere to Adam Smith's thought, gives a particularly stupid definition of value: "Value is what people believe it to be." What an idiot this Greenspan is! Poor Adam Smith. (Greenspan, *The Age of Turbulence*, 617).

9. For Marx and the mercantilists, see Georges Labica and Gérard Bensussan, *Dictionnaire critique du marxisme* (Paris: P.U.F, 1982), 740.

10. Smith, *Wealth of Nations*, Book II, Chapter 3. http://www.adamsmith.org/smith/won-b2-c3.htm.

11. See http://en.wikipedia.org/wiki/Variable_capital.

12. Smith, *Wealth of Nations*, Book II, Chapter 3.

13. Smith, *Wealth of Nations*, Book I, Chapter 8. http://www.adamsmith.org/smith/won-b1-c8.htm.

14. Smith, *Wealth of Nations*, Book II, Chapter 5. http://www.adamsmith.org/smith/won-b2-c5.htm.

15. Smith, *Wealth of Nations*, Book I, Chapter 11, Conclusion of the chapter. http://www.adamsmith.org/smith/won-b1-c11-conclu-

sion-of-the-chapter.htm.

16. Smith, *Wealth of Nations*, Book IV, Chapter 7, Part 3. http://www.adamsmith.org/smith/won-b4-c7-pt-3.htm.

17. This is true of Alan Greenspan, for example, who in his autobiography *The Age of Turbulence*, published in 2007, devotes seven pages of praise to Adam Smith, while "cleansing" his thought of any reference to wage labor as the source of profit, to the theory of labor value, or to class struggle (Greenspan, *The Age of Turbulence*, 338–44).

18. The International Workingmen's Association (IWA), also known as the First International, was founded in 1864, by Karl Marx and Friedrich Engels among others. It united "anti-authoritarian" collectivists (such as Mikhail Bakunin's international movement), Marxist collectivists, and mutualists (followers of Pierre-Joseph Proudhon). Political activists, unionists, and cooperativists worked together in this association. The First International was dissolved after the failure of the Paris Commune in 1871.

19. Written between October 21 and 27, 1864; First published: in *The Bee-Hive Newspaper*, November 12, 1864, and in the pamphlet *Address and Provisional Rules of the Working Men's International Association*. London, November 1864.

20. Jacques Adda, *La mondialisation de l'économie* (Paris: La Découverte, 1996), vol.1, 35.

21. Michel Beaud and Gilles Dostaler, *La pensée économique depuis Keynes* (Paris: Seuil, 1996), 32.

22. See John M. Keynes, *The General Theory of Employment, Interest and Money* (London: MacMillan, 1964), chapter 23 entitled "Notes on Mercantilism," where, like Marx, he emphasises the mercantilists' contribution.

23. See Beaud and Dostaler, *La pensée économique depuis Keynes*, 54.

24. Quoted in Beaud and Dostaler, *La pensée économique depuis Keynes*, 37.

25. Quoted in Beaud and Dostaler, *La pensée économique depuis Keynes*, 40.

26. Keynes, *General Theory*, Final Notes.

27. Charles-André Udry, "Los orígenes del neoliberalismo: F von Hayek: el apostol del neoliberalismo," *Desde los Cuatro Puntos*, no. 1 (1997)

28. Friedrich August von Hayek, *The Road to Serfdom* (London: Rout-

ledge Press, 1944).

29. Perry Anderson, "Histoire et leçons du néo-libéralisme: La construction d'une voie unique," *Page Deux* (October 1996).

30. Milton Friedman, *The Counter-Revolution in Monetary Theory* (London: Institute of Economic Affairs, 1970).

31. Beaud and Dostaler, *La pensée économique depuis Keynes*, 274–75.

32. Beaud and Dostaler, *La pensée économique depuis Keynes*,188.

33. Quoted in Pierre Salama and Jacques Valier, *Pauvreté et inégalités dans le tiers monde* (Paris: La Découverte, 1994), 149.

34. Ominami in Rafael Urriola ed., *La globalización de los desajustes* (Caracas: Nueva Sociedad, 1996).

35. Margaret Thatcher, *The Path to Power*, 1995; quoted in Udry, "Los orígenes del neoliberalismo."

36. Jack Hirshleifer, "The Expanding Domain of Economics," *American Economic Review*, vol. 75, No. 6, 1985, 53.

37. Joseph E. Stiglitz, *Globalization and Its Discontents* (New York: W W Norton & Company, 2002), 35.

38. Daniel Bensaïd, *Marx l'intempestif* (Paris: Fayard, 1995), 178.

39. Hayek, *The Road to Serfdom*, (96 in French ed.).

40. World Bank, *World Development Report: Workers in an Integrating World* (Washington, 1995), 104.

41. World Bank, *World Development Report*, 104.

42. World Bank, *World Development Report*, 95.

43. Quoted in Anderson, "Histoire et leçons du néo-libéralisme," 27.

44. http://www.doingbusiness.org/documents/fullreport/2010/DB10-full-report.pd.f
"Doing Business 2010" is the seventh edition of a series of annual reports on regulations that facilitate or complicate the practice of doing business. The report presents quantitative indicators on the regulations of companies and the protection of property rights in a comparison of 183 countries. Regulations having repercussions on ten stages in the life cycle of a company are evaluated: starting a business, dealing with construction permits, employing workers, registering property, getting credit, protecting investors, paying taxes, trading across borders, enforcing contracts, and closing a business. The data for "Doing Business 2010" dates from June 1, 2009. The indicators serve to analyze economic results and to determine which reforms were effective, and why. The 2010 report covers 183 countries.

45. "Doing Business in 2010: a record in business regulation reform," http://www.doingbusiness.org/features/Highlights2010.aspx.

46. Renaud Vivien, Eric Toussaint, and Damien Millet, "A Stronger IMF and Word Bank: Threats to People of Both the South and North," 12 October 2009. http://www.cadtm.org/A-Stronger-IMF-and-World-Bank.

47. World Bank, *Promouvoir le développement social. Contribution de la Banque mondiale au Sommet social* (Washington, 1995), 35.

48. George Gilder, *Richesse et Pauvreté* (Paris : Albin Michel, 1981), 127.

49. Thomas-Robert Malthus, *Principles of Political Economy: Considered with a view to their practical application*, 1820.

50. Greenspan, *The Age of Turbulence*, Chapter 25.

51. Greenspan, *The Age of Turbulence*, Chapter 23.

52. Greenspan, *The Age of Turbulence*, Chapter 19.

53. Just as a reminder, Myron Scholes and Robert Morton were awarded the Nobel Prize for economics for their options pricing model. LTCM (long term capital management), the speculative funds which they were advising, was on the verge of bankruptcy in 1998. Alan Greenspan was one of the main actors involved in the bailout of LTCM in September 1998.

Globalization from Christopher Columbus and Vasco da Gama until Today

1. This article is an expanded version of a talk given by the author in Kerala (India) on January 24, 2008 entitled "Impacts of Globalization upon Poor Farmers." Participants of this conference, a majority of whom were women issued from rural background, came in response to the invitation of the Santhigram association and VAK (member of the CADTM international network) within the framework of the World Week of Global Action launched by the World Social Forum.

2. One must add the Danes, who made some conquests in the Caribbean Sea, without forgetting in the North, Greenland ("discovered" several centuries before). As a matter of interest, the Norwegians had reached Greenland and Canada much before the fifteenth century. In particular, see the voyage of Leif Ericsson to the "Americas" at the beginning of the eleventh century (he moved from Labrador to the northern part of Newfoundland) where a colony was briefly established, forgotten for a long time, in the

Meadows Bay.

3. The name America comes from that of Amerigo Vespucci, an Italian sailor at the service of the Spanish crown. Indigenous peoples from the Andes (Quechuas, Aymaras, etc..) call their continent Abya-Yala.

4. Among natural resources, one must include the new biological resources brought back by the Europeans to their countries, then diffused in the remaining of their conquests and further: maize, potatoes, sweet potatoes, cassava, capsicum, tomatoes, pineapple, cocoa, and tobacco.

5. Figures concerning the population of the Americas before the European conquest have been differently estimated. Borah estimates that the population of the Americas reached 100 million in 1500, while Biraben and Clark, in separate studies, provide estimates of nearly forty million. Braudel evaluates the population of the Americas between sixty and eighty million in 1500. Maddison adopts a much lower estimate, assuming that the population of Latin America reached 17.5 million in 1500 and reduced by more than half, a century after the conquest. In the case of Mexico, he estimates that the population went from 4.5 million in 1500 down to 1.5 million one century later (i.e. a depopulation of two-thirds of inhabitants). In this article, we adopt the conservative hypothesis as a precaution. Even within this hypothesis, the invasion and conquest of the Americas by Europeans can clearly be counted as a crime against humanity and genocide. The European powers that conquered the Americas exterminated entire peoples and the dead can be counted by the millions, most probably by tens of millions.

6. The Spanish and Portuguese crowns who ruled South America, Central America, and a fraction of the Caribbean during three centuries used, as Catholic powers, the support of the Pope to perpetrate their crimes. One must add that at the end of the fifteenth century the Spanish crowns expelled Muslims and Jews (who did not convert to Christianity) during and following the Reconquista (that ended on January 2, 1492). Jews who did not renounce Judaism, emigrated and mainly took refuge in Muslim countries within the Ottoman Empire, which showed greater tolerance towards other religions.

7. From that point of view, the message of the Pope Benedict XVI during his trip to Latin America in 2007 is very offensive against the memory of the peoples who were victims from the European domination.

Indeed, far from acknowledging the crimes committed by the Catholic Church against indigenous populations of the Americas, Benedict XVI claimed that they were waiting the message of Christ, brought by the Europeans since the fifteenth century. Benedict XVI should answer for his words in front of the courts of justice.

8. From Asia, Europeans brought back the production of silk textiles, cotton, the blown glass technique, cultivation of rice and sugar cane.

9. Namely the famous Silk Road between Europe and China followed by the Venetian Marco Polo at the end of the thirteenth century.

10. Officially, Christopher Columbus tried to rejoin Asia taking the Western route but we know he hoped finding new lands unknown of Europeans.

11. Starting with the sixteenth century, the use of the Atlantic Ocean for traveling from Europe to Asia and the Americas marginalized the Mediterranean Sea during four centuries, until the boring of the Suez Canal. While the main European harbors were in the Mediterranean until the end of the fifteenth century (Venice and Genoa in particular), the European harbors open to the Atlantic gradually took over (Antwerp, London, Amsterdam).

12. See Eric Toussaint, *Your Money or Your Life: The Tyranny of Global Finance*, Haymarket Books, Chicago, 2005, chapter 7. The first international debt crisis occurred at the end of the first quarter of the nineteenth century, simultaneously hitting Europe and the Americas (it is related to the first global crisis of overproduction of commodities). The second global debt crisis exploded at the end of the last quarter of the nineteenth century and its repercussions affected all continents.

13. In coastal towns of East Africa, traders (Arabs, Indians of Gujarat and Malabar, and Persians) were heavily involved in business, importing silk and cotton fabrics, spices and porcelain from China and exporting cotton, wood, and gold. One could meet professional sailors, who were experts in the monsoon conditions of the Arabian Sea and the Indian Ocean.

14. Needham, 1971, 484.

15. In the fifteenth century, Beijing was connected to the areas which produced its food supplies by the Grand Canal which was 2,300 km long and was easily navigated by barges thanks to an ingenious lock system.

16. There have been many debates about European gross domestic

product (GDP) per head compared to the rest of the world. Estimates vary enormously according to the source used. Different authors, such as Paul Bairoch, Fernand Braudel, and Kenneth Pomeranz reckon that in 1500, European GDP per capita was no higher than that of China and India. Maddison, who strongly opposes this view (for underestimating the level of development in Western Europe), reckons that India's per capita GDP in 1500 was $550 (1990 equivalent) and that of Western Europe $750. Whatever the disagreements between these authors, it is clear that in 1500, before the European powers set out to conquer the rest of the world, they had a per capita GDP that was at most (i.e., according to Maddison's deductions) between 1.5 and 2 times that of India, whereas 500 years later, the difference was tenfold. It is quite reasonable to conclude that the use of violence and extortion by the European powers (later joined by the United States, Canada, Australia, and other countries with significant European immigration) were largely the basis of their current economic superiority. The same reasoning can be applied to Japan, but in a different timeframe because Japan, with a GDP per capita lower than China's between 1500 and 1800, only became an aggressive, conquering capitalist power at the end of the nineteenth century. From that time on, the growth of GDP was staggering: it increased thirtyfold between 1870 and 2000 (if we are to believe Maddison). This is the period which really made the difference between Japan and China.

17. See Maddison, 2001, 260.
18. See Maddison, 2001, 110.
19. See Gunder Frank, 1977, 237–38.
20. The Dutch did the same with Chinese porcelain production techniques, which they copied and since then present as ceramics, faience and blue and white Delft pottery.

The Market: The New Faith

1. Eric Toussaint has a PhD in political science. He is president of CADTM Belgium (Committee for the Abolition of Third World Debt, www.cadtm.org). He is the author of *Bank of the South: An Alternative to the IMF-World Bank*, VAK, Mumbai, India, 2007; *The World Bank, A Critical Primer*, Pluto Press; *Between The Lines*, David Philip, London-Toronto-Cape Town 2008; *Your Money or Your Life, The Tyranny of Global Finance*, Haymarket, Chicago, 2005. He has recently published *Un coup d'œil dans le rétroviseur. L'idéologie néolibérale*

des origines jusqu'à aujourd'hui, Le Cerisier, Mons, 2010, and *La crise, quelles crises?* (with Damien Millet), Aden-CADTM-Cetim, Brussels-Liège-Geneva, 2010.

The Irish Crisis: A Complete Failure of Neoliberalism

1. The present article is largely drawn from a slide show by Pascal Franchet ("Actualité de la dette publique au Nord", http://www.cadtm.org/IMG/ppt/Actualite_de_la_dette_publique_dans_les_pays.ppt).
2. The tax rate on company profits is 39.5 percent in Japan, 39.2 percent in the UK, 34.4 percent in France and 28 percent in the United States.
3. The problems experienced by the German Hypo Reale Estate (bailed out by Angela Merkel's government in 2007) and the collapse of the US business bank Bear Stearns (bought over by JPMorgan Chase with the help of the Bush administration in March 2008) were partly due to dodgy hedge funds located in Dublin.